Praise for Irene Silt

Praise for *The Tricking Hour*

"More than a polemic against work (though it is a very good one) *The Tricking Hour* is a meditation on what it means to process the world through your body; to feel life—love, loss, pain, ecstasy—to the fullest extent possible, all while knowing that your body is not (only) yours to control, that people with immense power get to dictate how you use your body, and thus how you experience the world. Silt writes compellingly about the issues facing sex workers, but their lessons about autonomy and pleasure under capitalism apply to all of us."

– P.E. Moskowitz

"These essays constitute a carefully and beautifully formed nebula of revolutionary thought and praxis. Silt's gorgeous synthesis is led by both righteous anger and gestures of deep care, born and fostered in spaces, booths, and backrooms both inconspicuous and flatly public. To encounter this missive is to encounter one of the truest manifestations of learning and living life past capital, past work's totaling reach, and into a life centered around love."

– Ryan Skrabalak

Praise for *My Pleasure*

"Irene Silt's My Pleasure tops from the underworld, where 'the inverse of pain / is in no way pleasure, it is acceptance.' Silt's poems wander straight into the throat of capital, purging loss in order to touch what we all must 'thrust aside / in order to live.' Desire spills out of Silt's mouth: jaw locked in exhaustion, where the trick and the lover blur in the direct address. Destroying time, rotting money, and leading us into the trenches of wanting, these poems are odes to the power of finding yourself flat on your back. Like the glow of a primal wound, Silt's poems teach us how to suffer—and how to love—more exquisitely."

– Rosie Stockton

"Irene asks, 'What if I am against boundaries?' and we are left with our limits. These poems bring us into the ecstatic tremors and absolute terror of self knowledge, all touch a violent mirror to the world and a flight line from the inflexible motions of capital. My Pleasure throws every possible angle of light upon desire so that we may see its shadow, honestly. What do we lose when wanting becomes having, when work becomes pleasure, when we are forced into the waning existence of escape? What do we win when we lose ourselves?"

– Nora Treatbaby

"We were being filmed as the twink rammed into me and my head hit the cheap tile wall of the fleabag motel's shower stall. There was something like an occlusion then, I worshiped his skin for the camera, and then my head hit the cheap tile wall again and again and so. I think of that sound as an evidence of what Catherine Clément would term syncope, an absence of self, and in Irene Silt's My Pleasure, the syncopic moment of rupture is ever-present. Silt's indelible book forms an argument that there is no stable subject—'the mulch fell away / in my arms was a large black snake'—but instead a porosity of subjectivity that is made most apparent in moments of fluidity, in fucking both as a means of survival and a means of battling hegemonic systems that attempt to master or explain every fissure, every tear. It also asks the questions, 'What might we want, when the wanting is finally able to dig in? What is deeper in life than just wanting to live?' And then the book answers itself: 'There is nothing in the world / to move a body but another body.' But do not be mistaken—Silt's is not a book about love, but instead a moving lyric treatise on the desire for liberation, a question about the boundaries of flesh and subject, and a positing that our desires are undefinable, as indefinite as ourselves, and as dynamic, like water. The book is sopping wet, dive in."

– Ted Rees

The Tricking Hour
By Irene Silt

DELUGE BOOKS

©Irene Silt, 2022
All rights reserved

Published by Deluge Books
info@delugebooks.com
New York / Los Angeles

Design and cover by Violet Office

ISBN: 978-1-7362104-5-1
Distributed by Ingram

1. THE TRICKING HOUR 11

2. QUEER TIME 16

3. SCREEN TIME 22

4. GESTURES OF REFUSAL 28

5. NOT YOUR CONSTITUENT 34

6. ON LOVE 40

7. FLOW STATE 46

8. SEX WORKERS AGAINST WORK 52

9. STIGMA 58

10. DEATH 64

11. FEELINGS 68

12. ACKNOWLEDGEMENTS 75

13. BIO 77

THE TRICKING HOUR

Time has never made any sense to me. Or rather, I am told the way I describe my experience of time does not add up. I am so disconnected from any common meter that I remain in disbelief of that sort of containment. I think this is what makes me a good whore.

When I consider my work, I think about many moments—self-timed photographs, waxing my cunt on a schedule, texting clients, doctors' appointments. When I describe my work, I speak in hours—my hourly rate, the hall of hour-long VIP rooms, the hour at which my friend should expect me to text to confirm I am still alive. We all want to know what we can get in an hour. They ask: what will we do? I ask: how much is an hour worth to you?—knowing that the labor in question could never be contained within a single hour, that no truth of worth will ever cohere.

Week to week, my body feels it has been doing sex work for varying amounts of time. In her book *Caliban and the Witch*, Silvia

Federici writes, "The body has been for women in capitalist society what the factory has been for male waged workers: the primary ground of their exploitation and resistance." I can only reconcile this confused feeling of labor-endured when I let go of linear time and the idea that we ever hold a job that has a discrete beginning and end.

The work is never done in a body separate from the one I spend my life within. When a client responds to an ad, the sex, the seduction, and the emotional labor I have done for most of my life becomes intrinsic to capital. Prostitution is the most obvious, basic work in the history of exchanging commodities. I have a visceral understanding of the use-value, or the want-satisfying power, of my service. Capitalism takes this value and makes it into mere work—an abstract labor force that needs to be managed.

The whores, the strippers, the dommes: we present a fathomless threat when we rise as an invisible class, for our work is both essential to society and continuously pushed to the margins. This work is crucial for many men you know, and is crucial to their deepest, most comforting secrets. A secret for the unloading of secrets, a service uncontainable. Our struggle is against stigma, that which keeps us in shrouded territories we all see, yet not everyone recognizes. Our liberation will not be reached through a permanent position in capital which capital can then exploit in more efficient ways. I do not want to be legalized. The work-regulating role of the state will always include policing workers on and off the job, and prosecuting criminal activity in all aspects of workers' lives. The more legitimized my labor becomes by the state and capital, the more I am forced to work. I want an end to criminalization, an end to work, an end to capitalism.

I am a sex worker primarily because of this position against work. The very word "work" disgusts me in an immediate way, like "police" or "prison." The police are an organized gang who rape and murder, who raid strip clubs and tell us we have no right to decency. Policing is most successful in its lack of boundaries, as it lurks in the strip club dressing room, in the security cameras, and as we act in fear, separating ourselves from the street hookers just a few blocks away in order to maintain a false sense of security.

Work is a class signifier people are asking you to disclose when they lazily ask, "What do you do?" My answer is fucking. My work is correspondence, conversation, drying tears, blow jobs, slow movements under red light, asking the right questions, and grasping for answers that lead us to the next action. My work is to extend possibilities. My work is a way to support and reproduce the rest of my life, which is identical to so many other lives, though the means are not valued or recognized as this elusive concept "work." Sex work positions me at times without a boss, with a schedule I dictate based on my needs, with more money than I thought I could ever amass, with hours that feel like my own, unmanaged. The longer I do this work, the more I opt out of all other work. My lawyer client warns me about the gap in my resume. This is not an admittance of no future: if I believe in the resilience and ability of anyone to survive, to transform, to exist in a new plane, it is the hooker. Rather, this is a cementing of refusal. For each hooker who dies at the hands of unrestrained misogyny or is imprisoned by the beaming spotlight of state violence, we continue to solidify our place here even if only for an hour a week.

This is not a glamorization of desperation, but rather a claim that all work in capitalism is desperate. Each time the state threatens me with regulations, I feel more desperate to do my work, before I am in prison or back washing dishes, back in school, back in a position of evaluating what I am good at, how else I have worth.

A lot of whore advisors warn not to bring up a customer's profession, because work is what we are all trying to escape through entertainment. But work is my favorite topic to discuss with clients. I have intimate access to a range of workers, professionals, and aristocracy, which grounds me in the shared delusion that is capitalism. Becoming vice is a relentless confrontation. I field the information of everything a person believes themselves to have, then find what they are lacking. I am paid to make up for that lack. I seductively assess whether I will be resocializing tendencies rooted in masculinity and alienation, or creatively avoiding hands grabbing at me. This violent vitality is easier to understand in certain moments than anything else in the world. I am not a therapist; I step into the black hole manifested by a lack of therapy. Tactfully, fueled by genuine interest, caffeine, and my need to reach some sort of understanding for how this market value will be determined, my client and I begin to exchange the absurdity of the worlds running parallel to the hour we have agreed to share—because my customer knows as well as I do that work never stops.

The tricking hour is every hour. It is when I walk to some businessman's hotel room with the sun looming over the casino and palm trees after a ten-hour shift at the strip club. It is at four in the afternoon as I meet my regular while he escapes his contracting job. It's whenever the doctor hits me up for a video chat in between his shifts. It's when things slow down and we get more intimate than we believed ourselves capable of. We encounter one another in the negative space of capitalism's schedule, the margins of standardized time. The vulnerabilities of the world become heightened: the vomit washing away on Bourbon Street, the desires hidden from your partner, my aching body nude and only as anonymous as the client is sane.

The way to help sex workers is to decriminalize the work responsible for releasing the tension of this brutal society which imprisons and murders our most prolific providers. Leave us alone. Sex work is at once a refusal and what is always there when the world refuses us. In an essay entitled "No," Anne Boyer writes, "a refusalist poet's 'against' is an agile and capacious 'for.'" The meaning, sound, and rhythm of my work simultaneously pulls me deep into my body while heightening my consciousness in outward vigilance. I go back for the money; I stay in the life when other options fall short. I am a whore because it aligns with my desire to refuse and reorder the world.

I am the glitter that distracts from the mold, the double-sided tape holding together the nuclear family, an emotional laborer with whom you have no shared investment other than the joy of sex and not being caught. Some days I am the last stripper to exit the club into the blaring sun and heavy air, crying with the roaring loneliness of the entire world. It is no longer the night before and it is absolutely not the next day. I feel purposeful in the work I have done; I feel right to have been paid; I question the dignity of a labor which is hidden away until it is strategic for city officials to shut it down. I fall asleep in my bed and am awoken, some hours later, by messages from friends, from clients, from lovers.

QUEER TIME

Do you think, in being a prostitute, I am selling my body? That I am transforming, compartmentalizing my identity, becoming Straight, becoming Woman, becoming (at one point of the day) something else in relation to the other bodies I am with? Do you think that I am performing more than you? That I am lying? The anti-sex trafficking propaganda seeps out of the public service announcement, occluding any firsthand accounts of sex work and silencing opposition with a cry to "save the children." There are multiple complications here, one being that my workplace is in fact my body, which I am rarely separated from, and that my body is never quite my own. My body is my factory. I am both the laborer and the commodity.

When I try to write about being gay, I think about my life so fully that I cannot form sentences. Being gay is an intrinsic and fundamental part of myself. Yet my queerness, like the rest of me, is in flux, constituted not only by myself but also by external forces—defined by cultural norms and expectations, by other people's projections and assumptions, by encounters with institutions of punishment and wellness. So my gayness is unimportant as well, lost in the constant doing and undoing of making contact with the world.

I do not feel differently when I am working. I feel in the same ways: I feel the dick I am fucking; I feel pleasure and pain; I feel empathy and rage. I feel gay. Sometimes, I slip deeply into vulnerability and expose myself as I always am, no matter who I am fucking or why. A man will ask: how often do you want to have sex with women? What toys do you use? Are you always this way? I pity these men who lay outside the queer unknown, who see women as a biological, static category. Women have sex with their entire bodies. When I am fucking a woman, I feel my body more fully and yearn for her body in a way that collapses the entire world into my cunt. I am full. I am inward, consumed by pleasure which unravels my need for a solid sense of self, my identity shattered as I am reduced to a sensorial continuum of my body, undone.

The conservatism of some women when it comes to sex work is understandable. These women are often exchanging sex for things less tangible than money, things like social capital and proximity to male power. Because those sex acts are performed under the guise or reality of mutual desire, they are less open to negotiation. I also have sex with men, out of both love and attraction. But having sex under any fixed social identity is always work: straight or gay, paid or unpaid. The more I have exchanged the performances of femininity, heterosexuality, and pleasure for money, the more I immediately connect the experiences to their many values. The exchange of money opens a space of possibility for sexual experiences that your partner might not desire themselves, for sex workers don't discriminate.

Essayist Pat Califia situates the sex worker in the realm of unapologetic deviant sex. Both queerness and whoring persistently resist the social order: reproduction, hetero-romantic monogamous love, purity, and citizenship. Sex as a profession makes me feel more queer than sliding my fist into my lover's orifice. I want you to know this feeling, when you are not simply colliding with another but integrating yourself into their core. My lover impresses upon me, as I impress upon them. Identity falls away when we are so brutally accepting of our bodies being in relation to the other. Yet identity builds itself right back up when I walk onto the street, forced to embody however I may be recognized. My queerness is not solidified by how I identify, how I look, who crushes on me. It cannot be articulated but only truly and constantly felt. It cannot be fucked into me or out of me. It is not an identity, but a disturbance of identity itself. It is the boundless pleasure that whores offer—cunts-without-commitment, while moving through underground criminal networks—that exposes the governing fictions which make up society.

I have always moved through different worlds and have passed through many lives. This is a common queer experience, or a common criminal one, born from a desire for both autonomy and community. These worlds and lives are concurrent, without beginning or end. The wife and mother class cannot recognize the whore class, leaving domestic laborers confused and underpaid, maintaining a verisimilitude of straightness. The mothers and wives who are also whores embody an even more intense web of secrets, providing for their families by superseding an economy built for the profit of men. Despite their industrious accomplishments, they are denigrated as whores, criminals who are paid for the same actions they perform at home. The criminalization of a whore's sexual encounter is another method by which the state destroys alternative forms of life. It is not me fucking the john that is threatening, as this arguably supports the institution of marriage. Rather, it is the exchange of money and the way of life—the autonomy and mobility that come with it—that cannot be tolerated. The criminalization of sex work operates in part to keep whores away from wives—two women fucking the same man on very different sets of terms. The possibility that these two classes would collude exposes the very contingency of women not demanding money for sex, for care, for emotional support, for all reproductive labor that capitalism depends on.

It's hard to know what disturbance, what criminal activity I am most invested in: queerness or whoring. I crave a large conspiracy of both, harmonizing, lustful, boundless—where feeling is everything, boredom and work nothing.

I have vowed to never purposely exit my body at work—in other words, to intentionally stop dissociating. Though on the other side, I realize I cannot exit whoring during the rest of my day. I wonder if I am closer to or further from rejecting the universal factory—the omnipresence of our work, of your work. The way that having a job transforms us into objects of mere existence, into commodities. I find myself and others confused by the multitude of signifiers I carry—often gendered by the features that my work necessitates, hailed by friends as femme for my smooth skin and pile of high-end hair products. Lovers hesitate to touch me to avoid reminding me of some unknown and supposed trauma. I end up more disoriented by the effect of sex work in the rest of my life than I am disoriented by the absurd performance of femininity and the labor of sex with cis men while working.

Work orders the rest of our life: our mornings, our vacations, our purchases, what we read, our care, our sex and pleasure, our home, the night. Even off the clock, my brain is fierce between the hours of 2 and 4 a.m., since this is the best time to sell VIP rooms. A factory is the time and space of our everyday subsistence. The repetitive motions and suppressed emotions of the strip club can at times feel more my own than those required of reproducing myself to move that way all night. Burn down the factory! Reappropriate the means of production! Is this place not my mouth which also eats, my hand which also flushes the toilet, my thigh which also presses against my lovers? I want all the whores to whisper ideas into my ear: our own advertising platforms, our own clubs, our own homes.

If my body is the site of my work, there is constant opportunity for sabotage. Frequently I don't even move, in my rejection of the eternal factory. I cannot adequately describe the pleasure in idleness on the other side of work, when I slip on my girlfriend's button-down back in the strip club dressing room, or when I lay naked in a hotel bed, finished with work but in the same exact sheets. My greatest pleasure is when I am with other sex workers and our loved ones, dreaming and preparing to revolutionize everyday life.

SCREEN TIME

The declaration that #sexworkiswork is all over Twitter and Instagram, on stickers and t-shirts. It's certainly on my mind, though not as an exclamation. It emanates, rather, from my sprained ankle, or from my rolling eyes as I navigate the ever-growing mess of my online presence.

Criminalized work in the digital age will spin you out. Multiple identities, accounts on five different platforms, emails, searching phone numbers of would-be clients, screening clients, sharing info about violent clients and time wasters, keeping a second phone in service, tax evasion… it's hard fucking work. #Sexworkiswork is a necessary call to make visible the substance of what we do, so that we may move toward control of that substance.

The work of sex has become obvious to me. I create content, stories, pleasure, ultimatums, comfort. I extract something of us and of this world to create the perfect iteration of love and lust for my customer. Sex, of course, is not separate from life; it is always at work in how we interact with the world and each other through economies of desire. The blockage so many people have to realizing this reminds me of how I feel about the Internet.

The Internet has always filled me with dread, frustration, and confusion. It has prompted more self-loathing than most mistakes or indulgences offline. When I am being reactionary, I want the Internet to be an entity that has nothing to do with me, though in reality it is included in every aspect of my life: to communicate, to obtain commodities, to learn how to use those commodities, for transportation, to watch videos of riots, to use for my work. Even a prisoner with limited or no access to the Internet is not removed from its totalizing grip on all planes of life, as imprisoned people receive money for their commissaries, earn rare email privileges, or have their identities solidified in an online database.

Computer programmers, like sex workers, are the intentional makers of what is perceived as unknown and inaccessible magic. In reality, this apparition is born only of our failure to understand the worker as one who embodies a technical mastery of a specific sphere of production. Imagine if those who write regulations were moved to fully understand the specificities of our work. Conversations might lead to the abolishing of patriarchal control instead of the criminalization of poor people who get tricked into giving a cop a blow job. If sex work was understood through the firsthand accounts and demands of sex workers ourselves, we would be significantly safer.

FOSTA (the Fight Online Sex Trafficking Act), a bill recently passed by Congress, is a blatant example of state regulations based in moral declaration coupled with disregard for the personal agency of people it claims to protect. This bill uses a deceptively noble title to roll back safe harbor provisions provided by the Communications Decency Act of 1996, meaning that online platforms can now be held responsible for the content generated by their users both in private lawsuits and in criminal court. FOSTA itself does not directly prosecute sex workers, but instead uses the threat of incarceration or massive fines to pressure online communities into censoring their users. Since FOSTA's passage, sex workers have lost the self-made online tools and practices which allowed us to dictate the terms of our workplace and move toward autonomous protection and collective power. Through forums for tips, lists of abusers, or advertising which asks for client screening, we became less isolated and safer—literally less likely to be murdered.

We cannot allow anything to become the exclusive terrain of elite experts, another tool of the state to control and capture us, another mechanism of fear and submission. The Internet doesn't belong to anyone. It is a completely decentralized system, similar to the rest of the world, in that it becomes what people contribute to it. There are free and open-source coders, there are content creators such as cam girls and radical news sources, and there are companies who commodify the Internet. The government wants us to believe that they have the ability to control how and why the Internet is used. Yes, the Internet is surveilled, partially funded, and regulated by the state. But like much else under capitalism, the state's control is not technical—it is through fear and commodification that this control is gained. The government may fund it, and corporations may own the material infrastructure of the Internet, but we make it. Our knowledge is the wealth of the working world, and we are dangerous because of that. Someone who knows how to make a system operate also knows how to sabotage it in an effective way or manipulate its functions to serve revolutionary ends. The collective force of sex workers and computer programmers links together skills and techniques that could be shaped into something other than systems of government. A programmer recently reminded me that the Internet works best when it is ungovernable.

Maintaining a secure internet presence is an important way to be an accomplice to sex workers. Everyone should take care to not expose their friends or colleagues to harm. An attempt to understand forces at play in our lives is an essential gesture of being part of a revolutionary force. The fight against the surveillance state is not born out of the issue of having "something to hide." It is a fight for the world we could create if we weren't being annihilated by multiple regulatory bodies to whom we are voiceless, excess bodies in a failing system. Between mistakes and panics, I have set out to understand the Internet more fully, to use it just as I would any public space—to live, to thrive, to meet, to get what I want. Here are some basic tenets I have learned along the way:

1. Compartmentalize your online activity. Keep separate devices for work and personal use. Success in this area makes remaining anonymous much easier, but remember this also relies on everyone you are communicating with to respect your anonymity.
2. Do not save passwords or use any autofill options. Use a different and complicated password for all your accounts, minimum eight characters, including numbers and symbols. You can save your passwords in a program called Keepass. Do not use Dashlane or Lastpass.
3. Update your devices. Stop clicking "remind me later."
4. Stay out of the DMs. Do not use direct messaging on social media to communicate about anything criminal. These areas are screened by filters and are under increased scrutiny due to FOSTA.
5. Research the Terms of Service (ToS). The super boring legalese when you sign up for a service just got a lot more interesting. The website tosdr.org highlights the most pertinent information that can otherwise be impossible to decipher in these documents. Use what you've learned in the ToS to clean your social media profile of any

keywords that might get you banned, shadow-banned, or flagged.

6. Use Signal, a messaging application for smart phones, for as much of your text communication as possible. Signal uses Public Key Encryption, which makes your messages unreadable to anyone but the agreed upon recipient.
7. Use ProtonMail for your emails. Before ProtonMail, we had to rely on PGP keys and other complicated methods for encrypted email conversations. Protonmail takes encrypted email communication, enhances it, and wraps it in an easy-to-use interface. It now even supports encrypted communications with email addresses that are not ProtonMail accounts. Use CAPTCHAs for verification, and do not set a recovery email. After you create an account, ProtonMail will send you notes on best practices. Their mobile app is considered safe as well.
8. Use a VPN on all your devices. Purchase using a gift card or Bitcoin. Always make sure your VPN is active when using your device and consider using your VPN's kill-switch if available. This will prevent your device from even connecting to the Internet unless the VPN is active.
9. Remove metadata from any photos. Taking photos from a cellphone or some cameras will embed a variety of information, from geolocation tags to user account information.
10. Turn off location services. Look through your phone's settings and turn off location services for all apps.

GESTURES OF REFUSAL

I have not been working nights for a few weeks, yet I still cannot sleep. I find myself awake, entangled in my sheets, rolling with the anxious, cyclical thoughts in my head. When I open my eyes, sometimes my hand is pressed up against the wall as if I am pushing my way out of something. Half of this dialogue is talking myself down. This is a time to rest, a place that could be safe from my conditioned counter-revolutionary consciousness. The rejection of conventions is a task which works itself out while I idle. My sheep-counting is an act of slow convincing. I insist—these thoughts cross a clear terrain: memories, traumas, and plans that are a means and an end. I am thinking of my gestures, or maybe our gestures. Stealing, acts of sabotage, fighting the police, going on strike. Self-evident gestures that do not need my anxiety to clarify their intentions.

The violence of extortion makes visible the value of labor. I learned this from prison rebels of the American plantation system. I am writing this shortly after prisoners all over the world took part in an organized strike from August 21 to September 9, 2018. Their gestures—work refusals, sit-downs, lockdowns, property destruction, retaliation—likely cost the system reliant upon their enslavement millions of dollars. This strike, called for by Jailhouse Lawyers Speak (an incarcerated group of prisoner rights advocates), is a prolonged struggle supported by comrades on the outside in an effort to win harm-reducing reforms, alternatives, and policy changes.

Prison rebels and sex workers inhabit similar corridors. Our labor is widely invisible to the market. We are criminals—meaning we are not able to be workers in legal or social terms. We cannot fit into traditional labor politics, or enjoy the prospect of a union and the legal protections it might provide. We are legally prohibited from communicating with others on our conditions or efforts; and even if we manage to, we are seldom believed and often brutally punished. Under the 13th Amendment, legally enslaved people are still growing our food and servicing my burner phone. Johns who are also cops kill sex workers in locked cars,* hunt us down at borders. Prisoners and sex workers have a shared need to destroy state power.

If there is a certain affinity that sex workers share, it is not nebulous, not a sisterhood or "the life"; it is a visceral knowledge of lawmaking's inherent violence. The rules and regulations that are billed as heroic protective measures create a deep strain in my chest, the same chest which is not mine at all—not mine to touch on a strip club stage, not mine to sell. What violence do we need to engage in to escape the expansive partnership of the making of law and that which conserves it?

Becoming a sex worker entails exposure to the exchange value of sex. We are already refusing the convention of the unrecognized, unquantified, and unlimited nature of the work of women. We make visible our labor value, and we make it apparent to those who seek our labor. More smiles? More money. There is a moment of satisfaction in this process that only sex workers truly know, though there is also a hollow solitude that we face on the other side of refusal. I cannot realize myself through work. I am simply provoking. How to escalate this provocation? How to induce a current out of these anxieties that could lead to a different reality, one characterized by (as Foucault theorized in *The History of Sexuality*) "sex without the law, and power without the king"?

The strip clubs on Bourbon Street become less and less tenable. We arrive at work and find our clubs closed without warning. How dare we feel stable, comfortable? Always have your bags packed; remember no one cares about you. The pang of stripper realities whips back around just as you let your hair down. It is when we are openly strategic and intelligent that we risk our livelihoods: strippers fight the city council to keep the clubs open and then have our contracts terminated for daring to approach a position of agency or solidarity. Organizing is only tolerated when it is in line with corporate interests.

Like most workers, strippers have a long list of grievances: contracts that keep us in a state of precarity, unsafe working conditions, busted equipment, the club making more from services than the providers ourselves, reducing our tips, house fees, discrimination by weight, age, race, and tattoos, "attitude," "appearance," pregnancy as grounds for firing someone, termination, cutting locks from personal lockers, bag searches, clubs sending in their own undercover "mystery shoppers," colluding with law enforcement. The precarity and transience of our industry necessitates cross-club and even cross-city lines of affinity in order to create leverage with our demands. Our organizing on Bourbon Street included hard lines against the police and positions against gentrification and sanitization of our city, against a city council that both dehumanizes and disregards our right to body autonomy, and against the attempts by the state, the Covenant House, and journalists to turn strippers and other Bourbon Street workers against street-based sex workers. We must continue to show up against brutality and coercion as shown in the raids of strip clubs on Bourbon Street and in New Orleans East, and the subsequent conduct of club owners who throw us under the bus to shift blame away from their own ineptitude.

There is a certain plowing of the sea in all these thoughts that herald my sleepless nights. We need a gesture that transcends small talk; we need to strike; we need to consider all the risks and shift our dependence on sex for our basic necessities to each other. Housing, food, childcare, our social lives—how do we reach common availability of basic needs, so that we feel stable enough to pull through something like a work stoppage? The state and anti-sex work feminists would like us to believe that we have made our own conditions, that our criticisms of the industry persist because of our inaction. We must also refuse a victory defined by adapting to the world, to their world.

My hand against the wall—is it for stability, in defense? It is not a reaction of fear for myself. It is a consideration of what is at stake. It is fear for comrades on the inside being put into solitary confinement for the content of their letters, for organizing. Fear for sex workers barely scraping by. One of the few truths I know is that we want to protect each other in an immediate way. The difficulty is in knowing that increased compensation will not destroy each apparatus of control, but only bind us tighter in dependence on them. It is not different, better work that I seek, and it is not rehabilitation. I am often at a loss, gagging when I honestly agree with many coworkers that stripping has at times been the only constant in my life. We enter through the club doors as our favored option for financial autonomy. What prevents us from being as resolute in regards to our working conditions as we are with a customer? Following the boldness of the prison rebel, I want to discover how to act despite isolation, violence, and constant surveillance; how to insist on a better life.

I need to think toward another gesture. Not the extortion of demands made against my manager, but a vision of my work without the labor relation. How do we use our bodies, each other, animals, objects in the world, without making claims of possession over them? How do we take our refusal so seriously that we do not return to business as usual—ever? No, not even off the job. A universal, permanent sex strike which is either species suicide or the end of gender itself? A refusal to be specific instruments, a refusal to be women, which will always entail the gender relation in which labor is carried out. A refusal of the abstraction of law. Sex without labor.

*We dedicate this column to the memory of Donna Castleberry Dalton, a 23-year-old mother of two, who was murdered as our last issue was going to print. She was shot eight times point blank by Officer Andrew Mitchell of the Columbus, OH police, within his undercover squad car, in an encounter wherein he had pinned his locks so she could not escape. On our minds also are Melissa Ramirez, Claudine Anne Luera, Ricky Janelle Ortiz, and Guiselda Alicia Hernandez, whose lives were stolen by Border Patrol agent/confessed serial killer Juan David Ortiz. May their memories be a blessing. May they Rise in Power.

NOT YOUR CONSTITUENT

This campaign season, sex worker rights and decriminalization issues—not usually a topic of mainstream discourse—made appearances in the platforms of politicians. Democratic Socialists of America (DSA) member Alexandria Ocasio-Cortez defeated longtime incumbent Representative Joseph Crowley in New York City in the primary fight for the Democratic bid for the House of Representatives, all while opposing the Fight Online Sex Trafficking Act and the Stop Enabling Sex Trafficking Act (known as FOSTA/SESTA). A catalyst for much above-ground organizing for sex worker rights due to its regressive criminalization of safety measures in the sex industry, FOSTA/SESTA has a growing body count. And though congressional candidate Suraj Patel went up against a FOSTA/SESTA co-sponsor and lost, my friends and I are still talking about his involvement in the first town hall meeting run by sex worker rights activists in Brooklyn, where he came out against FOSTA/SESTA. Another DSA member, Julia Salazar, who is running for a New York State Senate seat representing North Brooklyn, has had sex workers canvassing for her, highlighting her support of an existing bill introduced last fall that would repeal a loitering law used to arrest sex workers. Salazar has also condemned massage parlor raids and came out against prosecutors' ability to enter evidence related to sexual history in rape cases (as it stands, prior prostitution charges may be brought up as evidence to discredit a rape survivor).

Finally shedding summer's torpor, November has always felt full of combustible potential, yet there may be no better fire extinguisher than a polling station. Electoral campaigns are ruthless black holes for grassroots and autonomous movements. Lifetimes of work, of fighting, of dying, are distilled into the act of voting, a sacrifice of your present convictions and desires for a promised hopeful future. All the nuances—the rages, the struggle—are flattened into an issue on someone's platform, an interactive link on a website. We are made into constituents, an integral part of the violence that establishes and constitutes the law, the stamp of approval in the name of democracy. We cast our votes; our choices now belong to the politicians to make what they will of them. The politicians are on the other side, telling you what to do, as you voted them to do so. This is a fundamental aspect of democracy: organized power over the masses. You cannot protest this by voting; voting is bound up in these fundamentals. There is no way to abolish State power through democracy. You cannot vote against voting.

We see a hollowing out of movements by politicians year round: for example, the ongoing movement to abolish Immigration and Customs Enforcement (ICE), which gained visibility this past June. Occupations outside of ICE facilities sprang up all over the country in protest of the many horrific actions of ICE, including separating immigrant children from their caretakers while awaiting deportation. People gathered and erected autonomous spaces, built barricades, fed each other, fought the police, and lived together for a moment—all under the shared understanding that we do not need or want the State to deport people.

Ocasio-Cortez demonstrated a politician's power to co-opt and neutralize this abolitionist movement, which many of her supporters were part of, with a tweet in August: "#AbolishICE means not having an agency that incarcerates children and sexually assaults women with impunity. It does not mean abolish deportation." And thus abolition was redefined as reform. We must demand to know what a candidate like Salazar truly means by decriminalizing sex work, lest she joins Ocasio-Cortez in a politician's sleight of hand. The policy platform developed by sex workers for Salazar includes meaningful positions; it is sensible for anyone to agree with them and a fine reason to wind up at a ballot box—but what is down the line? Nicer police officers carrying out deportations, harsher stings to get to the true exploitation of the sex industry? If abolition to one DSA candidate means reform, what does decriminalization mean to another?

The idea of a town hall meeting in a dimly-lit strip club in the middle of the day sounds weirdly magical, and I am inspired by the efforts of sex workers to be seen, to lead conversations against stigma, to exist without apologies. Power is not actually something that can be represented; power exists through its wielding, through its use and effect. The claim of representing others is a wonderful career option, but freedom cannot be gained by proxy. The very existence of a class of politicians is proof of our disenfranchisement. When we place our horizons on candidates to create options for us, we relinquish control of our communities. No more ceding our labor, movements, passion, skill, bodies to a class of experts. We must set the possibilities, and create enough capacity to make the changes we need directly. The politicians can catch up on their own.

Why cooperate? Since when do whores collude with the State? If I am to collude, it is with those who don't have the option to vote—the undocumented, the felons, the houseless, those killed by police. It is as if we believe in the power of politicians so much that we want to be them. We are groomed to believe that voting gives us a voice and control in how we run our lives. Perhaps the more privileged among us sex workers—those of us who are white, who work indoors—turn to voting for some semblance of power, through controlling the lives of people we may otherwise rarely interact with. Democracy is the infrastructure created to flatten difference, to maintain existing power structures in the crisis of capitalism with glimmers of change, channeling our energies away from the activities that actually make up our lives.

We cannot be made into a constituency. We are not a static, homogenous group. Our power is in part built through collective, material, and political organization. Yet my nausea in reaction to the Sex Worker Lobby comes from feeling that organizing is also necessary in the singular, in experience, in our sensibility. It is without this feeling that we decide there is nothing else but to fall back into the economy, into politics.

I do not believe that one comes out of a life of sex work unscathed. We understand sacrifice, understand that our decisions and lives are real enough not to fuck around with. I am not interested in making any of these apparatuses of control operable; I am not interested in measuring a movement's productivity in the realm of politics—I want to engage in a tradition of inoperativity. Whatever grease I have left sure as hell is not going into making the Democrats slide around easier.

My frustration is not with Salazar, or the vibrant sex workers organizing for her. Capitalism reduces existence into a slow process of debasement. Voting is more degrading than most choices

I am presented with. We can live our lives waiting for solutions in order to face this degradation, to ignore the melting ice and the migrant bodies washing ashore. Reformism is a rubbing off a ruin—it gives no form. It reminds me of the third hour of trying to get a client off after he's done too much cocaine. We need something more than relations, more than deals—more than moving from wound to wound until they are something presentable to the public for consumption, an issue to vote on.

The nowness of my work is incompatible with representation. It is larger than the future, a now which holds more weight and more potential than any long term plan, any goal, any investment. Of course sex workers can get voter turnout. We are incredibly good at reading a room, very convincing, and often create the realest intimacy people experience in their day. This is possible through perception of the now, of exactly what is taking place, a perception more decisive than knowing the distant future in advance. This allows us tact in survival, de-escalation, community, our way of doing things. These skills I am presenting are valuable; they are earned, honed. Giving them to politicians is a weighted decision. I believe we live communism through deploying and deepening an ensemble of ties, not through working to ensure the existence of any specific entity. It is through life itself, not something outside of us, of me. Let us collude with the comrades before us—Black and trans sex workers who know this system must burn down along with the State's idea of the complete ego, of perfectly unified selves. We must remain unsurprised when the State's long-awaited solutions inevitably include our extinction.

If we weren't cyclically interrupted by the trappings of election seasons, maybe we would see our own autonomous power flourish. Eventually, Bernie Sanders will be dead like all the prostitutes that died after he voted in favor of FOSTA/SESTA. His supporters will have to think of a larger question—not what gets the people out on Election Day, but what the fuck happens when we lose? What happens after we accept that the same democracy that facilitated the rise of fascist regimes is not a system capable of saving us?

ON LOVE

There is a group of women in New Orleans known as the Church Ladies, who walk down Bourbon Street to share the "love and freedom of Christ" with strippers. They pray, sometimes come into the clubs, give us roses; beyond this, I am unsure what they do. One night, they gave me some hand soap and a small card with a Bible verse on the back, which I found to be a deeply inspiring text describing my work:

Are you tired? Worn out? Burned out on religion? Come to me. Get away with me and you'll recover your life. I'll show you how to take a real rest. Walk with me and work with me—watch how I do it. Learn the unforced rhythms of grace. I won't lay anything heavy or ill-fitting on you. Keep company with me and you'll learn to live freely and lightly.
(Matthew 11:28-30)

The card has been on my vanity mirror ever since. When I read it, I see my limbs in blue light. I hear my voice in the hollow of a man's neck, my hand sliding down an arm, to a wrist, to a thigh, then to myself. We are in contact. I can even smell the club a little bit. It is true and it is love.

At times, I feel so close to my memories of love—the way it felt, how the lighting was, the variety of food I was consuming and how often, the scents and the mess of time. The way time and bodies fold repeatedly into themselves, until a lack of separation is revealed. Visually, I remember my lover's elbow, or their diaphragm. But in my body I revel in the unforgettable achievement, the confusion and exhilaration of refusing to live beside ourselves. That time when we became indiscriminate from everything around us, making our way together, when your thoughts made mine more clear.

I believe in the sad dissatisfaction of the couple, yet see no escape route in denouncing it as a social form. The couple is forced to stand in for desire itself, so that we learn to stop yearning; we do not reject unlivable situations; we do not annihilate what has captured us. But by love I do not mean the rules of relationships. Not the order of things, but vast playfulness, unscrutinized. I do not mean: what are my morals concerning fucking, or how will everyone deal with me loving many people, deep and uncontrolled? Not who you have as a lover, or who you allow to have you, or what it is you do with them, and when. But how we experience love, how love passes through you, how you let love tear you apart and knit you back together as something that truly makes sense in the world—no longer as an amputated, isolated subject. We do not suffer from being individuals. We suffer from trying to be that. I mean fucking love, its transformative power, the only thing for us.

It has been so easy to be overtaken with the pain and degradation of life. To confuse love with a crisis. I worry about my individual capacity, about focus and productivity, about the work I need to be doing. Sometimes I think money is the only way I can care for people; sometimes money is the only way I could care for a person. I think, how will this end—before I have been invited for a beginning. I have feared: to be in love is counterrevolutionary, a distraction, a whirlwind of relations that even at its best is suffering. I can see in my customer's eyes—the only thing worse than the fact that I do not truly love him is the unimaginable tragedy that would follow if he truly loved me.

But it is love itself that undoes this lie that we are rigid individuals, vessels holding a discrete life, separated from other discrete lives. That separation is contrary to life—a disorienting estrangement, giving up contact with oneself as well as with the world. You can resist all feeling this way. Maybe you were vulnerable with someone once, but she doesn't talk to you anymore. You fall numb. Well, a stripper can grasp you from the inside. She has done it to me. She asked me, can I kiss you on the mouth? Will you let me take your body in sin, will you come with me? Out back, to know about my many minor lives and what could have been. In seconds, I fell in love. I have returned to this love for weeks.

We are all so fucked up that its horror has become mundane. I know my work drains me, because if I stay awake for too long afterwards, I begin to see my nightmares on repeat. I do not think about the unrelenting, assaulting fingers and the spit; I think of bad memories unrelated to work. When I grab a stranger by their insides, I find an unorganized chaos of forces: bits of experience, fragments of meaning, flashes of grief, moments of jest, deep hatred, whatever is left when they lose control in a way they did not expect—whether from exhaustion or from trust, maybe from alcohol. I see myself all along the perimeter of the club, in the mirrors reflecting our fragmented world.

As a child, I loved in order to escape abuse. I loved in search of a sensuality I was never introduced to, to learn a new language.

I have fallen in love under the specter of prison, in times of police raids and bail bondsmen at 2 a.m. and winter air that thickens even more as it cools down. In the heaviness of my own incarceration I have allowed myself to be loved, honest about not loving the same way, but receiving that love nonetheless, allowing myself to be open to impossible joy and care. We will constantly be undone and shattered by love. Desire will be choked out of us by the State. We are not free, but love is the clearest way to visualize freedom.

In this moment, I want to vomit out of me all love, to rid myself of love so that I can see it, make it material. I am crying because I have been dumped and I have broken things off; I have fallen in love with the same person multiple times and I have known she causes me more subtle pain than I can take and I have learned and I have lied. The relationships I have had with these people I am in love with, the devotion and the depth, approximates the kind of relationship I want to have with many people, with tasks, actions, regions, my body, places, tools, cuisines—with all the things that make up a form of life.

When I ask you all about love, I hear mostly how you need it. You tell me what you have learned from the pain, about the loves who have died and how you still feel them. You asked, what else could there possibly be to do?

I can settle into this: that we are for love. That we are against those who are against love. Isolation is the trap of capitalism, not the frivolous exchanging of valentines. Being alone in your refusal is a trap. We are not against Valentine's Day, only that it exists on one day. Maybe we are against a singular Valentine. When I am working a lot, I feel further from being in love. I start to grasp for it, create it in desperation with the wrong object. I know I am so proximal to it that I experience it, though each night I pile up intimacy so fast that I forget most of it.

I am hesitant to write that I experience love in the strip club. Even though I am not looking for love, it really is in there— I need only to grab you from the inside, to undo you. It undoes me. We do not need to remain numb. We can allow ourselves to be cracked open. Knowing this arousal is the very practice that will allow me to stop going to work, to learn to take what I need. To find freedom in pleasure: to be fucked by exhaustion, fucked by leaving your pimp, by rupture, by forcing others to bear witness, by freedom young and old, by the silence of estranged lovers, by forgetting, by the return, by excess.

I have experienced more sadness through love than is comprehensible. That is the proof of it being an experience, after all, that we are not just beside each other, but becoming together. Separation always occurs, and we feel something leave our bodies. We will rest in each other, then attempt to live freely and lightly.

FLOW STATE

Our bodies are present for all of the simultaneous lives that we live. Despite its fragility, our body is our constant in all situations. The sex, the substances, the dancing, the struggle, the stress, and the scrutiny press against my body whether or not my mind decides they count. What happens to my body in the strip club never stays in the strip club. The body is there before consciousness thinks it.

Whoring is a constant experimentation with the deep unknown of the body. My body in contact with other bodies, in contact with itself, moving in places deemed unconscionable and in ways it is forbidden to do so. I know the power of what a body can do, and am constantly in awe of what occurs when I slide into an optimal state, pushing beyond my known limits. The mind is unaware of the procedures of the body, the body is unaware of thought. The unconscious of the body is a realm we rarely dare to explore.

Many of us practice active dissociation in our work. We see it as a powerful tool that allows us to protect ourselves from anything that threatens us. We daydream while at our dishwashing job, or detach from our pain receptors, no longer reacting to the blisters from our tools. Sometimes I dissociate to cope with a touch I do not want to feel. I start singing along to the song playing. Sometimes I dissociate at work to escape the pains of the rest of my life. It is at times the only way to get through a job, and at times a perfectly harmless tool if I can maintain some control over it.

Personally, I have always wanted to be further inside my body, to be put back into my own body. Long before I was a sex worker, I needed to touch other bodies so that when I touched mine I knew the difference. To press upon saplings, boulders, leather furniture, the pavement, bodies hard and soft, seeping and unstable. To experience enough to know what joins my power, and what diminishes it. To be part of a greater flow, to dissolve boundaries between myself and the world.

After years of sex work burnout and related injuries, I began training in martial arts as a way to re-enter my body. I have been training in Brazilian jiu-jitsu for about a year. Jiu-jitsu is a grappling art, like wrestling, where the fight is brought to the ground and a power struggle is played out until submission. It is premised on the concept that any body can defend itself against bodies that are bigger or stronger, through technique, leverage, and frames. A frame is a part of your body that is used to create and maintain space, relying on your skeletal structure more than muscular strength. They are obstacles that you place in the way of your opponent's body to restrict freedom of movement, like your knee pressed up upon their chest.

The mental toughness required of sex work is layered. Teasing that toughness out of coping mechanisms to move past dissociation gives me balance and, potentially, a more full life. Jiu-jitsu is a self-care practice that orients me toward survival. Through it I gain physical strength and stamina through motions I find deeply therapeutic. Grappling gives me the feeling of moving my hips, face, hands, elbows—all of my body—in similar ways as in other situations, but for different reasons. It teaches me to do with my body what I have wanted to do in so many other moments: to take power. Jiu-jitsu has also brought me structure, helping me to regulate my sleep schedule as I switch from nights to days. It gives me a place to go, an entire world to escape to where I rarely dissociate, as success is only possible through fully inhabiting my body. It is an avenue toward flow state.

The psychologist Mihály Csíkszentmihályi popularized the concept of flow state to describe complete immersion in an activity, where the ego falls away and time feels different. It is beautiful improvisation: every action, movement, and thought follows effortlessly from the previous one. Your whole being is involved. You are in the zone, hustling with a remarkable ease. You find and expand the cracks of all false boundaries surrounding you. You are beyond control, wild yet with intense clarity. It is a light breaking-and-entering of desires no longer distant.

Normally, we process the world through language. We turn life into data. We are preoccupied by the need to understand things in a particular way, unable to apprehend anything immediately. We are constantly surrounded by ideas, notions, things to conceive, things to form—so that at any moment all action is rendered impossible. How do we escape the overwhelming feeling of being surrounded by things outside of ourselves, looming in our minds, waiting to be interpreted?

Flow state is the ability to inhabit an area of action through the continuous postponement of reason, an area outside the failings of cognitive understanding. It is joyous, self-forgetful involvement through concentration. It is bliss. There are many triggers and iterations of flow state, as you might know, but for me the most profound is the merging of action and awareness. My actions are one with direct perception, feeling in the moment, a cognition made apparent not through my mind, but rather my actions. I can act creatively, when earlier, I could only attempt to process.

In practice, jiu-jitsu changes a situation so that it favors the defensive player. It trains you to be comfortable under duress. It is about creativity, openness, the unconscious ability of the body, muscle memory, and fluid motion which adjusts quickly when new challenges arise. Strength is used only when you are too late to intuit the movement of your opponent's body. Strength and hardness are secondary to pliancy and the freshness of unrestricted being. When we harden, we tire and we die.

After sparring with my coach the other day, he told me I had good transitions. I thought of all the transitions I had with my client just before class, where my intimacy was seamless. Each touch, laugh, or word spoken came effortlessly from the last and was met by the instant feedback of my client's mounting desire and joy. Instead of dissociation, my mind and body achieve a parallel. Surviving looks and feels effortless to my opponent. I was not an actress, but rather able to truly act in a way adequate to my situation.

Sex workers too must seize the advantage through form and situational strength. As in jiu-jitsu, we must use frames. Screening, largely considered a best practice for prostitutes, requires a john to provide personal information or a reference from a provider to indicate that they are not law enforcement, otherwise dangerous, or a waste of time. We must always create a scenario weighted toward us. This is the active thrust of autonomy that criminalization will always destroy. We ourselves are familiar with the multitude of energies around us; we know our life and who intersects with it; and we alone can do the things that keep us safe, because only we understand the specific world we operate in.

When we are forced into a specific relationship with our clients by externally-imposed legal structures, we learn nothing but obedience. We are crushed by our lack of power, all under the auspices of safety or public health. I have worked under an array of conditions, rules, and regulations, but never in a decriminalized environment. It is the State, rather than my clients directly, which has always left me the most vulnerable. But outside the scope of a controlling apparatus, we can set our own parameters.

It is this situation, when we begin from a place of all possible relations, that produces the highest motivation to relate to me in a positive way. If I am laying out the terms, I maintain control, and the john is motivated to ask in a way that I might respond "yes." When the State is laying out the terms, I am forced to begin with a "no." All the techniques I learn, all the leverage I create for myself, all the frames I put between myself and my clients for protection are withered away by the legal frameworks limiting the possibilities of my body. It is the external refusal presupposing my own which provokes the john himself to pull my g-string off without asking.

Flow state is desirable because it approximates life without this externally imposed suffering. I want everything to collapse onto itself, my mind no longer conceived as a self-contained field, substantially differentiated from my body. I want full clarity of intention, given to me through action. To be free from conceptual labor. To build my own capacity. Flowing in jiu-jitsu allows me to function and operate consistently upon life, with it and through it, not through referencing good or evil, right or wrong, not according to a rule or law. In jiu-jitsu, the diversity of life and the particularity of life's non-linear sequences leads to my creative force. I am not thrust outward from my body, torn apart or caged. I am folding into myself.

SEX WORKERS AGAINST WORK

On June 2, 1975 over one hundred prostitutes occupied the Saint-Nizier church in Lyon, France, to demand the end of fines, strike back against police violence, and demand the release of ten sex workers imprisoned for soliciting. This occupation is commemorated for its fervor to end stigma and demand better work conditions each June as International Whore's Day. This month, I am passing along a text written by sex workers in a clandestine whore's network. It is a call to the militant spirit of the occupation in Lyon. It is also a response to the lack of anti-state and anti-work discourse in sex worker organizing. We will all be punished for gaining autonomy from the state until the state no longer exists. Our wager is that truly autonomous sex worker organizing is integral to an anti-capitalist revolutionary horizon.

Right now, we are a handful of whores attempting to put our position into words and our words into action. In the time we have been in the sex trade we have seen and learned a lot. We have witnessed the shift toward strong identification with the term "sex worker" and even pride in the labor of selling sex. We have seen platforms flourish for sex workers to find work or to find each other and develop communities. We have seen less shaming and less fear of being judged in radical circles, and even the development of a niche popularity that celebrates sex work as a more desirable option amongst relatively few or less desirable options.

Although many of these changes are beneficial, they are not without criticism: whorephobia is still the pervasive view of sex work within society as a whole, especially if you are poor, working class, Black or brown, or trans. The whorearchy amongst sex workers continues to reinforce this trend, as stripper chic and other forms of non-sex service providers place themselves above other workers who fuck for a living. We see white cis women who have built marketable personas with relative ease as high-class escorts or sugar babies take the spotlight as voices for the sex worker movement with open admission about their lives, while others are left concealing their every move, leading high-risk double lives. We have seen an expansive activist and online community turn into a demand for recognition and protection by the state, for legislation and elections to lead the way to "liberation."

We do not believe our liberation will be reached through a permanent position within capital, to then be exploited in more efficient ways. We do not want to be legalized. The regulating role of the state will always include policing workers on the job and off-work, and prosecuting criminal activity in all aspects of workers' lives. Work is not something that confines us solely as we labor in a building or room. Work orders the rest of our life: our mornings, our vacations, our purchases, what we read, our care, our sex and pleasure, our home, the night. The more legitimized our labor becomes by the state and capital, the more we are forced to work. We want an end to criminalization, an end to work, and also an end to capitalism altogether.

A narrowed and flattened lens into headlines such as "Eight foreign nationals freed from sex-ring-massage-parlors in Berkeley" can only illuminate what one is already able to understand of the complex components of this "sex ring." Immigration, inability to find work, racism and misogyny are all factors at play in governances' so-called victories against human trafficking. Raided strip clubs and massage parlors turn into Airbnbs. Every strip club's "If you see something say something" anti-trafficking posters suggest we dial 1-800-XXX-X-ICE. These are not heroic efforts to save "vulnerable women," but methodical avenues of gentrification, capital development, and, ultimately, violence against sex workers and their loved ones.

We cannot wager on the acceptance of sex work, or for those who are obsessed with our condition to change our realities. The anti-human trafficking movement (a multimillion-dollar industry) is a macroaggression waged by every arm of the state and its collaborators: NGOs, religious organizations, racist and authoritarian feminists, ignorant or opportunistic do-gooders. It thrives off modernity's humanitarian lust to save the young and vulner-able, shaped by decades of unearthing—and consequential sensationalizing—of global capitalist horrors. We think of its lethal predecessor, the war on drugs. In these spectacular wars, we witness the unification of both the left and right wings of the capitalist state who, together, design these mechanisms of control in order to extract wealth from vulnerable populations just finding ways to get by. The savior brigades, the Drug Enforcement Agency, the whole carceral system, negate the possibility within informal economies to escape poverty and degradation.

If the challenge was to force our representatives to recognize our humanity, we would be front row at all the city council meetings. But we know their wealth depends on controlling us. Their role is to bring us back into their world, when we have spent our lives creating our own against all odds. To wait until our suffering is recognized through constructing audible narratives for our enemy's consumption is to take away the power that already exists in our history of struggle.

We are against both economic exploitation and state regulation of economic exploitation. Because of this, we are necessarily for our own autonomy. This is something we must develop together. Let's evaluate the limits of reform and assimilation while honoring the legacies of sex worker struggles, and move beyond more institutionalized sex worker activism.

We would like to prompt a conversation toward a more thorough understanding of how sex workers, marginalized yet certainly not marginal, can organize material solidarity and care networks that build community while also undermining the state's ability to hold us hostage in its many ways. We believe being a sex worker is a powerful shared experience wherein our natural inclinations to survive outside of the state's control and oversight have the potential to manifest incredibly powerful care networks, as well as confrontational responses to those who harm us.

We believe it is crucial to criticize our subjectivity as sex workers and acknowledge that not all who sell sex identify that way. We maintain that our unique experiences, as those with the experience of sex for survival, leaves us—and us alone—capable of recognizing our limitations, traumas, tendencies, and sensibility toward liberatory relations. Beyond misrepresentations, false glamorization, and weaponized stigma, the wisdom and navigation of those who sell sex to live give a critical perspective for the many more who are fighting for freedom from work and from the state.

We acknowledge and honor the hard work, risks, and death endured by many over the past century in order to create a framework for the sex worker-specific organizing and political analysis we use today. The struggle of sex workers and the longevity of our struggle relies on our ability to continue the militant practices of the Black radical tradition, to stand in solidarity with those defending their indigenous land from pipeline development and other state-sanctioned genocidal expansions, and to remember that the hope for queer liberation was fought against the police in a riot at Stonewall by Black and brown trans women, prostitutes, queens, dykes, and other gender traitors. We refuse to let these daring, courageous moments of our legacies be distorted and rewritten into playbooks for passive resistance. Today solidarity means: fight back.

STIGMA

Sex work has given me so much. I first turned myself out because I needed money, in a john's house in a suburb that I can't remember the name of. Every day since then, I have been grateful to have money, my basic needs met, and a body that exceeds my expectations of resilience. I am overcome by all the other things I've learned—about the world, the place I live in, its geography. Overcome by the slow accumulation of friends who exchange sex for money, who lay awake with me when I can't sleep, who can keep up with the endless torrents of disasters, bliss, bastards, harm, and elation that sex work entails, unperturbed by the mystifying awe of our situations. In cars or walking down the street, we speak of the untapped well of all we have witnessed—the wonder, the body knowledge, the wisdom we might not have wanted but would never give back.

I wish I could speak without fear about the ways sex work has helped me feel whole in my body—its fleshly goodness, pliable, strong, a force I've sculpted—and about the ways I feel disgusted and confused about my body, how I fantasize about pulling my tits off my chest, about the failures of my body and the way I have deformed it.

I wish we could talk of all the things we can endure for an hour, about building trust in a given period of time. About food and how it moves through us, psychosomatic phenomena, hallucinations from exhaustion. I wish I could give you an analysis of political tendencies within a strip club, about international solidarity and communiqués, about anonymous literature that cuts so deep we mourn the loss of all the journals we burned in shame.

I have learned about the manipulation of bodies. About seizing what is yours, giving away excess, about how she escaped, about vigilance, self-responsibility, and motivation. About counting, escalating goals, wrapping money, rotting rubber bands, decoys. About freedom and what it means, what it could lead to. About owning property, destroying property, communizing it, giving it back, about settling up right with ghosts. About cultures, customs, and comfort, about nostalgia and memory and intoxication. And about survival, every whore's driving concern.

I liberated myself from the idea of limits, but I am not naïve enough to forget that I risk my life for that liberation. I want to have these discussions with others, with all my friends and lovers, with my comrades. I want what we have learned, what we know, and what we do to be communicated to all, to enrich our lives through both the positive and negative realities of sex work.

With all this knowledge, we could have a better understanding of surveillance, racism, the police and what they do with their guns, of labor unions and their failures, of the moralism and emptiness of political parties, of reform, of the idea of respectable employment. We could be more effective crossing borders, evading law enforcement, resisting paying taxes; at horizontalism, hiding, and self-defense; at helping our friends leave abusive relationships, at planning assassinations, at resisting careerism and other bourgeois aspirations. We could move past the romanticism of the working class, of the noble proletariat.

But these discussions remain only between sex workers because of stigma. Stigma, the mark of shame, creates and permits public and private disgrace, discrimination, and disapproval. Stigma produces your identity for others to interpret, informs the way all others will relate to you, regardless of any reality of your situation, your options, your choices, your own will. It can control your relationships, your housing, your connection to your family and your children. It justifies your murder, your torture, your erasure because the stigma predates your corporal body. It creates the conditions for the codified maltreatment of sex workers, drug users, people with varied abilities, gender nonconforming people, people of color, migrants, the endless list of deviant populations, contrived to maintain dominance and order under capitalism.

Perhaps the most obvious force of stigma is the law. Laws make it extremely difficult to sell sex and be protected as you might while selling almost any other commodity. The Fight Online Sex Trafficking Act (FOSTA/SESTA) recently brought this legal dimension to public attention when it criminalized measures (such as online screening and bad date lists) that sex workers used to be safer and to secure higher pay. Stigma relegates us to the margins to keep our dirtiness away from clean families and neighborhoods, even when they were our families and neighborhoods to begin with. Laws make us vulnerable. Laws put prostitutes in outdoor cages where they die of exposure, like Marsha Powell during her 27 month sentence after offering a cop a $30 blow job in Arizona. Laws turn humans into wasted bodies. There is a police code for crimes involving marginalized people—gang members, prisoners, prostitutes—NHI, or No Human Involved. That code appeared on the police report for Marsha Powell.

In New Orleans and everywhere else, stigma creates the opportunity for the rich to get together with the cops and religious organizations against whores, performing their moral panic around sex and vacating buildings to make room for Airbnbs all in one fell swoop. In a New Orleans City Council meeting in March of last year, then-Council Chair Stacy Head dismissed the concerns of a room of sex workers: "I believe in child labor laws and the EPA and that puts people out of business sometimes." There is no "Green New Deal" for prostitutes within the swirling force of stigmatization—of white supremacy, cis-heteropatriarchy, poverty, prison, drugs, debt, mental illness—all the realities that land us washing dishes, cleaning toilets, sucking dick. Our dead bodies serve as justification to fund vice units and special task forces, full of cops like the one who killed Donna Dalton and assaulted at least two hundred other sex workers in Columbus, Ohio.

Once, I turned around and saw a crowd of people running in fear of being shot in the strip club. I saw strippers being shoved to the ground, tumbling over with the tables, rolling ankles in their clear heels next to broken clear glass. I saw all the men who ask what is a beautiful girl like you doing here, men who will defend a woman's honor—the same men that go to war—pushing past strippers as if we were lifeless sandbags to take the bullets. I hid in a closet. Another stripper was crying, "No no I have children, I cannot die." I told her we wouldn't, but I was looking at her naked body, thinking about my naked body on the table at the morgue, my g-string being slipped into a plastic bag.

I also know a more intimate world of stigma among the well-intentioned, where sex work is no big deal, something neutered, happening somewhere around here but still separate. Existing in this world relies on the maintenance of the "happy hooker" vibe, or of total secrecy. Maybe there is a fascination, a cultural obsession, a playfulness in the perceived glamour. An obsession with money, what sex acts are worth, what you are worth, and what's it worth to you? Was the money good?

In the moments that I would like to spend outside of the structural othering I experience, I find myself stifled, unable to adequately express my joys or sorrows. Friends may acknowledge that stigma exists, and even champion "sex-worker representation," while still only accepting the love and care of a whore on the condition that the whoring remains elsewhere. Friends can only accept whoring as a clean and concise economic experience that fits into their questions of worth, as if there is an acceptable logic to our bodies doing work for money. A whore must be skilled enough to extract money from a multitude of situations, and then turn around and explain on command what was earned and how, and what was sacrificed in the earning, all to friends who want to make sure you know that they could never. My existence is only legible through horror or glamour, not the same complex brutality as your particular hustle. These interpersonal disappointments are not mistakes, they are actions informed by tired ethics and the inherited unease of sex—by stigma.

Sex work helps me try to use my life in a way I find meaningful. I find my work extremely challenging, difficult, and at times consuming. I also have more control in my pursuits than ever before. I am in the position to support myself and others. I can show up, contribute to communist experimentation, do research and writing, spend time considering my health. I often do these things and still question it all on the other side, due to the disappointment and anxiety from the creeping stigma all around me. The complex realness of sex work is undeniable. I want a world in which all sex workers can translate that realness, to crush stigma and all the ways it is weaponized against us.

DEATH

When I think about sex work, I do not think about sex. I think about bodies. I reflect on what bodies can incite in other bodies. The fascinating powers of our physical forms—generating repulsion, awe, devastating lust. I try to wrap my head around the opportunity to touch and be touched in the ways our bodies yearn for, not in order to become a more skilled prostitute, but to understand the powers we can harness from our bodies that are so easy to forget about. I know we gain power from what we are proximal to. I think about the unmappable force which becomes thicker through proximity to death.

Doing sex work has been a natural progression in my life. It has never been taboo. This is inextricable from my relationship to my mother, who has been disabled for the duration of my life. In the week following my birth, we were separated, and when we were reunited later that year, she was without the brain tumor we had grown together. My understanding of existence was formed by the intense risk of producing life, the miracle of non-death, and the continuing challenge of maintaining both. We do not enter the world alone. Our becoming and consciousness is miraculously happening with and simultaneous to the deterioration and recreation of life around us. Not unlike the tumor, I am a substance both of and out of something living.

I have spent time maneuvering my mother's body, reattaching to it in order to move it, to pick it up, to loan energy or stability. I have spent my life in unshakable anxiety, listing in my head the consequences of time, addiction, misogyny, use, and neglect. I feel her pain and degradation as my own. Our relationship is defined by visceral observation, shared experience of the horrors of domestic life, substances and violence, and the wearing out of our bodies by patriarchy and capitalism—more than any practices of mothering or contrived family bonds.

I feel close to my mother in a way that is without spoken language. Her cognitive disabilities have evolved in unison with my abilities to express and analyze. She became sober when I was an adult, after I was already settled into a reputation of mysteriousness and flight. In my personal life, I am notoriously hard to access, to get a hold of, to touch, to schedule. I have never believed that a given set of terms should come with birthing a child. True love, non-obligatory intimacy, trust, and care are not gestated with a fetus. We have to be intentional in our material practice of deepening the skills in the labors of love.

Death work is mostly relegated to those who also experience it the most: marginalized workers. The thing with death is you can't leave it alone. It must be tended to. We do work around the loss of a body, the temporality of death, how it can reorder our lives, the arrangement of things. Around property and resources, and the responsibilities of other bodies. In the presence of death we depart from our dominant conditioning. Death alters environments. Energy is released, our bodies are transformed into vessels for new things. Death prompts new modes. We are more open to what could be put to use, less beholden to illusions that typically structure our day. A death dispels the fog of business as usual. It can even embolden us to finally have adequate responses to our world, as I learned from the riots in Ferguson and Baltimore, from the militant action of indigenous land defenders, from the Women's Protection Units in Syria, and from autonomous efforts in the wake of environmental disaster—in the wake of mass migration from once abundant corners of the world now extracted from or bombed beyond capital's use.

Death, when tended to, is transcendence for all who are in contact with it. We at once shudder and sigh with memories of a certain body connected to a certain mind, and then participate in its catapulting separation—the projection of that being's consciousness, through our labors of love, onto the life we create. We can see ourselves in the life around us, see the duration of the world, know it exceeds our singular bodies. When we are more than just something to take care of, and rather involve ourselves within a network of care, we can soften the finitude of the phenomena named death.

I am both haunted and blissed out by the slowness of death. My life began from the expulsion of living organs out of living organs. Something gushing, vital, so soft and vulnerable. And I recall moments where things have quickly hardened: my mother's varying paralysis, my own body in stress, the bodies of my dead friends, of strangers whose deaths are without consent made so public: victims of police murders, of war, of imprisonment, of exposure to the elements, ground down by work or lack of work. Our bodies processed as profit until they no longer exist. I try not to turn away from this world which produces death more systematically than it allows for life. I revel in the capacity I have maintained to be in contact with others, to soften. I am brought to my knees in front of all the sex workers that move in and out of this undoing, of being undone, of being so goddamn hard in this world but also providing, providing, providing. A body in use has an undeniable warmth. Our incomparable resiliency is formed through closeness to the real.

Every experience in sex work is fundamentally related to commodity. Our other relation is to the act of refusing to exist in the control and captivity laid out for us. We gain power in securing a beneficial, lucrative transaction, maintaining our safety to the best of our abilities. We get away with something. So it is like all other forms of work, but it is also distinctly different. There is something unspoken. This transaction changes our relationship to the confinements of all our bodies—gender, what goes where, what is what, who is meant to be in a certain place at a certain time, how we find joy and satisfaction, being filled up or filling up.

I am not thinking about a john penetrating me, or penetrating a john. The hookers I know and work with do not conceptualize themselves as giving sublime therapy, and johns are not rendered queer by the illegality of buying sex. It's just sex. But also, sex is everything. Sex work is the cultivation and manifestation of affects, the dichotomy of experiencing and witnessing ecstasy and boredom, pleasure and distaste, our bodies encountering each other for reasons and in ways that we are taught are wrong. In sex work and death work, there is no turning away; it is relentless confrontation. There must be an abundant well of power, filled by the body's need to create an intensity or trajectory—a thrust which functions to deepen. Not a release or escape from reality, waste, blood, the State, from the psychological disease of misogyny, from anger. Sex is a zone of potentiality. We leave the symbolic realm of language, of law, of identity, and we embody the real. The question is not: what is powerful about the experience of prostitution? It is: what will we do with the force we have cultivated?

FEELINGS

I invoke others to feel what I resist in my own life. Right now I feel, all at once, everything I put aside in service of survival. I have met disgust and love with a blank face. I allow nothing to pass through me, in and out. These feelings cling to my body. I wash them off my skin in the shower, but the drain clogs and I am staring down at gray water.

When one is possessed by anger there are distinct signs: a stern stare, red face, hurried walk, hair standing on end, unintelligible speech. Self perversion of the distraught mind makes the air itself menacing, gloom falls over everything. Anger is demanding, meant to be seen. The repulsion others feel in the face of my anger is palpable. I have so much.

But when I work I am powered by a different energy. I arouse defensive behaviors. I am calm and slow, disarming and gentle. I guide and comfort, present myself, wet. With masterful suppression I am unaffected by all that is presented to me. I collect my cash prize as a soft agent of attunement.

Sex workers deal in the proprioception of attunement and emotional sensing of others. This is the source of our power, knowing rhythm, affect and experience by close contact with others. To reach further than empathy to create a dyadic experience of unbroken connectedness by providing a reciprocal affect. The other source of our power is doing this outside of social norms or recognition.

I store my anger in my hair, long. I let it down, it does some of the work for me. Silent, to be admired. I would like to cut it off, but it has not worn out its use.

Mostly, when I wanted to lash out, I didn't. We will make the mistake to continue with the unbearable so that we can avoid reflection, work more as a way to not think about working. I visit man I hate after man I hate. I am here because I have worked too much. I have allowed my disavowal of limits to be mixed into the accumulation of wealth. The deterioration of my mind concurrent with that of the earth. I am debased at the same rate life itself is debased, and by the same conditions.

I have pressed my heel into a man's neck, dug my fingers into a sternum, open-handedly struck a face in the darkness of a lap dance booth. Afterwards I had no satisfaction, weighed down with fear the club manager would hear of what I had done. Nauseous as a jolted client comes back the next night, trailing me in silence, texting me threats. My violence met with more violence. I may be justified and righteous in revenge, but it does not alleviate the fight or flight drive. I return to the feeling of inhibition, losing authentic experience with the world.

My madness shows itself to me when I cannot see anything. I look at a painting, the sea, my lover, and my anger betrays me. All that is alive reminds me that I am a ghost. Madness shows that I am not what I used to be. I am disgusted with my anger, it cannot go anywhere it is meant to go.

Living requires criminal activity, with life being so crushed by power. Whoring came to me when I failed background checks. I know how to move through this terrain, make gains, shape it to my own choices. But how do I reckon with the concessions I have made for money? The work pervades my life, I can smell it on me. See it in the things I do, how I transport myself, where I sleep, what I eat, how I look.

I am exhausted. I have done this long enough to know that he will be waiting for my moment of weakness. When I put his name into the blacklist search, I saw no results. Really, he had so many entries, so many aliases in so many cities, that I mistook what I saw for the whole list, which in the twisted nature of industry, meant nothing for all it omitted. The list is not information until its stakes are registered as specific.

When I opened the door to his gaunt face and eyes, completely clear, I experienced the confusion of seeing nothing in the face of everything. I kissed him. The motion I am so well trained in.

Feelings have become something intolerable. My heart is in my mouth and I grow tired of myself. I must be ill. We know that fear produces flight, anger a rush. My decision to stay in the same embrace has planted a pit at my core, in defiance of regulated response patterns. I hate myself for every time I stayed, knowing that I stayed for the most rotten thing on earth. There has to be more than putting money to use.

I have had a man inside of me, inches from my face, putrid smell or expensive cologne, and wanted to scream in his face. Wanted after the deep sound you emit into a canyon or at the ground after collapsing in despair. I've had pain radiate from my cunt all the way to my throat, raw skin and tight hips. Wanted to choke and knee him, say no. But I didn't, I took the money.

There is of course an erotic pretense for violent ideation during sex. The hate fuck. The insane explosivity fueled by rage. Rage against him, rage for our sake. He comes to me corrupted by work, and I continue the pattern with mine. Workaholics are always the most deranged. They pay for resonance, needing the structure of the work relation and mediation of money to create a place of hiding. Proximity to this drains my power. I feel his deadness in my mouth in the cab home alone, I drink in the bath to forget his misery. Sensation titrates an experience, I am not ready for a full on catharsis.

In my work I have illuminated a path, offered expertise that adapts to each moment we are in. To pull emotions down from the ether, into now. To play with those emotions and illicit bodily reactions I can't summon for myself. Paleness, bursting into tears, lust, deep sighs, sudden flashes of the eyes. To relinquish. Underneath identity, the impulses of my body.

I use my body to transform another person's relationship to their social identity. This is a step out of empire and into life. Off the rock and into the water. To hold their insides in your palm, feel them explore whether or not they are you, you are them. To change a power dynamic before the determination of a subject and sense, a temporality starting up again in the midst. A relation arrives that is not based on identification or recognition but encounter and new compositions. I look for this association in sex, abstract concepts, new techniques, ambitious dreams, in the river, with all that is oriented toward the need for revolution. To experience again, everywhere, when the police were the ones running from us. Here is love, a life-making activity.

I experience these impulses in writing, through which I began remediating my relationship to want. The inability to act in the moment has made me, at times, unable to rouse anything to action. I desire unclouded and distinct action. My love and devotion to sex workers has shown me that this is our nature. I did not know gentleness until receiving the affection of a whore. Nothing has been more vicious to me than my own anger. I extend my hand from an arm of ambivalence, I do not invite the burden of hiding, I am relieved to have this out in the open. Take it, onward.

ACKNOWLEDGEMENTS

The Tricking Hour was originally published as a monthly column in *ANTIGRAVITY* from June 2018 to October 2019 under the name Saint Agatha. It was first compiled into a pamphlet by *TRIPWIRE* in 2020.

I give my gratitude to the sex workers who have influenced my thoughts and life. Many conversations and shared experiences led to these words. I did not write this alone. Boundless appreciation to *ANTIGRAVITY* editor Beck Levy who made *The Tricking Hour* possible and cultivated my work to completion. Thank you KO'S, Jay, Cass, Slee, San, Lyn Archer, April Showers, Les, Paul Torino, RJ Smith, The Clandestine Whores Network, Luce, Yoann, Chloe, David Buuck and Other Weapons Distro. My love to Rosie, Willa, and Cyrus who encouraged this new life for the essays and to everyone at Deluge who brought it to fruition.

Thank you to the Gulf Revolutionary Artists Formation, for producing pamphlet versions of the first five essays.

"Feelings" appears in Issue 34 of the *LARB Quarterly*.

BIO

Irene Silt writes about power, anti-work feeling, joy, and deviance. Their essays and poems have been published in *Mask Magazine*, *ANTIGRAVITY*, *Spoil*, *LESTE*, *Trou Noir*, *Poiesis Journal* and in the *Tripwire* pamphlet series. They live in New York.

Also From Deluge Books

Mercury Retrograde
A Novel by Emily Segal

Black Venus Fly Trap
Poems by Jeanetta Rich

Amor Cringe
Fiction by K Allado-McDowell

My Pleasure
Poems by Irene Silt

delugebooks.com

www.ingramcontent.com/pod-product-compliance
Lightning Source LLC
Chambersburg PA
CBHW071122030426
42336CB00013BA/2170